Navigating Your Own

DIVINE DETOUR

A companion journal

Navigating Your Own

DIVINE DETOUR

A companion journal

LORI ANN WOOD

ST JOSEPH, MISSOURI USA

NAVIGATING YOUR OWN DIVINE DETOUR: A COMPANION JOURNAL
Copyright © 2022 Lori Ann Wood

Paperback ISBN: 978-1-936501-82-3

All rights reserved. No part of this publication may be reproduced or transmitted in any form or by any means, electronic, mechanical, photocopying, recording or otherwise, without written permission of the publisher. Published by CrossRiver Media Group, 4810 Gene Field Rd. #2, St. Joseph, MO 64506. CrossRiverMedia.com

For more on Lori Ann Wood, please visit her website, LoriAnnWood.com.

Editor: Debra L. Butterfield
Cover Designer: Tamara Clymer
Cover Photography: Photo 217824013 © Konstanttin | Dreamstime.com

Printed in the United States of America.

Contents

Letter to the Reader 7
Day 1 - A Season of Grief and Gratitude 9
Day 2 - Soft Endings 13
Day 3 - Home or Him? 17
Day 4 - Sinking into the Mud 21
Day 5 - Learning to Lament 25
Day 6 - The Presence of Absence 29
Day 7 - Survivor Guilt 33
Day 8 - Waiting for Glory 37
Day 9 - Utility Room Faith 41
Day 10 - Holding Loosely 45
Day 11 - Anticipating Bad Days 49
Day 12 - The Size of Loss 53
Day 13 - What Lasts Forever 57
Day14 - Surviving a Collapse 61
Day 15 - A Prodigal's Parent 65
Day 16 - What Love Looks Like 69
Day 17 - Adjusting the Font Size 73
Day 18 - Mundane Matters 77

NAVIGATING YOUR OWN DIVINE DETOUR

Day 19 - Mosquitoes, Martians, and a Trustworthy God.................. 81
Day 20 - Both Sides of Water 85
Day 21 - A Lapse of Faith 89
Day 22 - Recency Syndrome 93
Day 23 - Locust Years.. 97
Day 24 - Languishing & Loaned Words 101
Day 25 - In the Shadow of a Stump 105
Day 26 - Finding Answers in Unanswered Prayers 109
Day 27 - A Better Memory 113
Day 28 - Getting Okay with Giving Up 117
Day 29 - When God Disappoints 121
Day 30 - Trust Enough to Surrender 125
Day 31 - Sitting on the Bus 129
Day 32 - Not What We Expected 133
Day 33 - In Between.. 137
Day 34 - Midrace Joy... 141
Day 35 - Making Mistakes.. 145
Day 36 - Parented by Porchlight 149
Day 37 - Conquering the Stairs 153
Day 38 - When Doors Close 157
Day 39 - A Desperate Reach 161
Day 40 - A Charge to Keep Questioning.. 165
About the Author 169

Dear Reader

This journal is designed to become your story. While my memories, journal entries, and questions in *Divine Detour* were a starting point, now it gets personal. For each day on the journey (which may for you represent a weekend or a week or even longer), I hope you will examine your unique trek with God and feel empowered to ask your own hard questions.

As I mentioned in *Divine Detour*, I didn't plan to keep a journal of any kind. I never wanted to relive the pain we were going through. And I certainly didn't want to give it significance. But after some encouragement from my husband, I started keeping lists at first, then poems, quotations, song lyrics that spoke to me. Eventually I wrote down some angsty communication with God that I wasn't even sure could be called prayers.

Those reluctant words became the basis for my Divinely Detoured Ministry and my first book. And from comments I've received from readers, it seems God had a plan to use them for good—as He so often does with the hard parts of our lives.

I wish I had written more, questioned deeper, and started earlier. But we can only change where we're going, not where we've been. That's true in life and in faith. So I am hoping this journal will help you take the first step toward embracing your own uncertainties and writing your own story, even if you don't feel ready. Not for the purpose of publishing, but for the purpose of flourishing. That's what I want for

NAVIGATING YOUR OWN DIVINE DETOUR

your faith and mine, despite the detour each of us may be on.

I've included some starter questions and quotes to help you remember my thoughts. I've also included Scripture to take you back to God's promises and character. From there, I'm leaving it to you. I hope you will venture out, even on what feels like wobbly scaffolding, knowing that questions build faith and God is waiting for you to ask Him.

Feel free to skip around and read and reflect where your questions take you.

The pages, like our footpaths of faith, are undated.

With you on the journey,

Lori Ann

DAY 1

A Season of Grief and Gratitude

Grief and gratitude can coexist, and maybe they have to. Maybe we can never appreciate fullness without loss. Maybe they are actually partners in bringing the realization of God's mercy into our hearts.

1. What is the most challenging takeaway from "A Season of Grief and Gratitude"?

2. How does "A Season of Grief and Gratitude" help you answer the life question, Is this life all there is?

NAVIGATING YOUR OWN DIVINE DETOUR

3. "A Season of Grief and Gratitude" explored the Question of Worry as it relates to processing loss. What other questions does this bring up in your detoured walk with God? What question keeps coming back? What question or unexplained event is standing between you and God?

4. Was there a time you felt alone in your grief?

5. Looking back, how did God come alongside you?

6. How would your faith be stronger if you knew God always sees you in your grief? How would that look in your life?

GO DEEPER

Read John 13:7, Luke 1:34, 46–48.

DAY 2

Soft Endings

Grace allows us to take risks with our faith and invest fully in imperfect people. And, perhaps most miraculously, it urges us past regret by extending God's costly pardon to ourselves.

1. What is the most challenging takeaway from "Soft Endings"?

2. How does "Soft Endings" help you answer the life question, Is this life all there is?

NAVIGATING YOUR OWN DIVINE DETOUR

3. "Soft Endings" explored the Question of Worry as it relates to regret. What other questions does this bring up in your detoured walk with God? What question keeps coming back? What question or unexplained event is standing between you and God?

4. Was there a time you felt captive to regret?

5. Looking back, how did God release you from regret?

6. How would your faith be stronger if you knew God extends grace without limit or qualification? How would that look in your life?

GO DEEPER

Read James 4:14.

DAY 3

Home or Him?

It's a difficult question to face: Is the idea of heaven to complete our desires or to complete our God? Maybe it is to fully align the two. Maybe it is to make God the complete desire of not only our afterlife, but also of our current life.

1. What is the most challenging takeaway from "Home or Him"?

2. How does "Home or Him" help you answer the life question, Is this life all there is?

NAVIGATING YOUR OWN DIVINE DETOUR

3. "Home or Him" explored the Question of Worry as it relates to meaning in the afterlife. What other questions does this bring up in your detoured walk with God? What question keeps coming back? What question or unexplained event is standing between you and God?

HOME OR HIM?

4. Was there a time you felt drawn to heaven for its reward alone?

5. Looking back, how did God pull you into a relationship with Him instead?

6. How would your faith be stronger if you knew God is the ultimate reward of heaven? How would that look in your life?

GO DEEPER

Read 1 Corinthians 13:12.

DAY 4

Sinking into the Mud

In choosing us, God often gives us more than we can humanly handle so we will lean on Him instead of our own imperfect power. He knows we can become too intent on our own knowing, our own impact, our own significance in the story.

1. What is the most challenging takeaway from "Sinking into the Mud"?

2. How does "Sinking into the Mud" help you answer the life question, Is this life all there is?

NAVIGATING YOUR OWN DIVINE DETOUR

3. "Sinking into the Mud" explored the Question of Worry as it relates to powerlessness. What other questions does this bring up in your detoured walk with God? What question keeps coming back? What question or unexplained event is standing between you and God?

SINKING INTO THE MUD

4. Was there a time you felt powerless to change your situation?

5. Looking back, how did God call you to lean on Him instead?

6. How would your faith be stronger if you knew God uses our weak moments to display His power? How would that look in your life?

GO DEEPER

Read 2 Corinthians 1:8, 12:9.

DAY 5

Learning to Lament

Lament shows belief like few other expressions can. In fact, it may be one of the truest forms of praise. Lament reaches out for Him when logic urges us to run away.

1. What is the most challenging takeaway from "Learning to Lament"?

2. How does "Learning to Lament" help you answer the life question, Is this life all there is?

NAVIGATING YOUR OWN DIVINE DETOUR

3. "Learning to Lament" explored the Question of Worry as it relates to our belief not matching our experience. What other questions does this bring up in your detoured walk with God? What question keeps coming back? What question or unexplained event is standing between you and God?

4. Was there a time you felt betrayed by the God you believe in?

5. Looking back, how did God meet you in this feeling of betrayal?

6. How would your faith be stronger if you knew God invites our expressions of lament? How would that look in your life?

GO DEEPER

Read Matthew 26:39, 27:46.

DAY 6

The Presence of Absence

A wise anonymous writer called *saudade*, "the love that remains." Despite the loss, regardless of the holes and amid the ache, the genuine love of saudade never leaves.

1. What is the most challenging takeaway from "The Presence of Absence"?

2. How does "The Presence of Absence" help you answer the life question, Is this life all there is?

NAVIGATING YOUR OWN DIVINE DETOUR

3. "The Presence of Absence" explored the Question of Worry as it relates to living with loss. What other questions does this bring up in your detoured walk with God? What question keeps coming back? What question or unexplained event is standing between you and God?

4. Was there a time you felt a gaping hole from something missing in your life?

5. Looking back, how did God urge you into embracing the ache?

6. How would your faith be stronger if you knew God intended the ache of saudade to point us toward heaven? How would that look in your life?

GO DEEPER

Read 1 Corinthians 13:13.

DAY 7

Survivor Guilt

Our God is a God of healing and restoration, sometimes here on Earth, but always in heaven. A medical cure here may grant us more years in this life, but not actually more time, because we have already been given eternal life. All of time belongs to believers.

1. What is the most challenging takeaway from "Survivor Guilt"?

2. How does "Survivor Guilt" help you answer the life question, Is this life all there is?

NAVIGATING YOUR OWN DIVINE DETOUR

3. "Survivor Guilt" explored the Question of Worry as it relates to the unfairness of life circumstances. What other questions does this bring up in your detoured walk with God? What question keeps coming back? What question or unexplained event is standing between you and God?

4. Was there a time you felt physical healings were doled out in an unfair way?

5. Looking back, how did God work through the circumstances of those not healed?

6. How would your faith be stronger if you knew God is always a God of restoration, whether here or in heaven? How would that look in your life?

GO DEEPER

Read John 11:4.

DAY 8

Waiting for Glory

The weight of glory is to be connected to God and yet realize its inevitable incompleteness in this world. To be immensely happy and still missing the most important part of your soul. *Sehnsucht* is finally having the very thing you had so desired and realizing that it was not what you truly wanted at all. That your soul longing involves so much more than you can plan or control or even comprehend.

1. What is the most challenging takeaway from "Waiting for Glory"?

2. How does "Waiting for Glory" help you answer the life question, Is this life all there is?

NAVIGATING YOUR OWN DIVINE DETOUR

3. "Waiting for Glory" explored the Question of Worry as it relates to feeling incomplete during our times of joy. What other questions does this bring up in your detoured walk with God? What question keeps coming back? What question or unexplained event is standing between you and God?

4. Was there a time you felt something missing even though everything was going right?

5. Looking back, how did God use that weight of glory to draw you toward Him?

6. How would your faith be stronger if you knew God intended for our best days on Earth to still feel incomplete? How would that look in your life?

GO DEEPER

Read 1 Corinthians 4:17, 1 Corinthians 2:9.

DAY 9

Utility Room Faith

When we open up to the fear and reality of dying, we are freed from the bondage of carrying the heavy unknown. Recognizing our inevitable death releases us to live rather than constantly preserve and protect. As we move from defense to offense, we shift our focus from escaping demise to encountering the Divine.

1. What is the most challenging takeaway from "Utility Room Faith"?

2. How does "Utility Room Faith" help you answer the life question, Is this life all there is?

NAVIGATING YOUR OWN DIVINE DETOUR

3. "Utility Room Faith" explored the Question of Worry as it relates to the fear of death. What other questions does this bring up in your detoured walk with God? What question keeps coming back? What question or unexplained event is standing between you and God?

4. Was there a time you felt fearful of death, for yourself or someone you love?

5. Looking back, how did God ease you out of this fear?

6. How would your faith be stronger if you knew God intended for us to encounter physical death yet still live on after it? How would that look in your life?

GO DEEPER

Read Heabrews 2:14–15, Ecclesiastes 5:15.

DAY 10

Holding Loosely

Against our nature, God calls us to hold our blessings loosely: jobs, health, relationships, family, financial security. To unclench the white-knuckle grip on these things, and cling tightly to Him. Hold everything (and everyone) else loosely.

1. What is the most challenging takeaway from "Holding Loosely"?

2. How does "Holding Loosely" help you answer the life question, Is this life all there is?

NAVIGATING YOUR OWN DIVINE DETOUR

3. "Holding Loosely" explored the Question of Worry as it relates to uncertainty in life. What other questions does this bring up in your detoured walk with God? What question keeps coming back? What question or unexplained event is standing between you and God?

4. Was there a time you felt the tendency to clutch something too closely?

5. Looking back, how did God place an unexpected blessing in one of your open hands?

6. How would your faith be stronger if you knew God gives us blessings to hold for a season and to release in another? How would that look in your life?

GO DEEPER

Read Job 1:21, John 3:16.

DAY 11

Anticipating Bad Days

God will call every one of us to exercise our mustard-seed faith along an impossible path in the coming year. On some pain-filled days. We can expect it.

1. What is the most challenging takeaway from "Anticipating Bad Days"?

2. How does "Anticipating Bad Days" help you answer the life question, Is this life all there is?

3. "Anticipating Bad Days" explored the Question of Worry as it relates to unexpected bad days. What other questions does this bring up in your detoured walk with God? What question keeps coming back? What question or unexplained event is standing between you and God?

ANTICIPATING BAD DAYS

4. Was there a time you felt slighted by God on a bad day you weren't expecting?

5. Looking back, how did God use that bad day to give you something more permanent to cling to?

6. How would your faith be stronger if you knew God uses bad days to change and refocus our hearts? How would that look in your life?

GO DEEPER

Read Matthew 5:45, Job 2:10.

DAY 12

The Size of Loss

L oss makes us all part of the same divine story in distinctive ways. Even when our loss seems humanly insignificant.

1. What is the most challenging takeaway from "The Size of Loss"?

2. How does "The Size of Loss" help you answer the life question, Is this life all there is?

NAVIGATING YOUR OWN DIVINE DETOUR

3. "The Size of Loss" explored the Question of Worry as it relates to loss in the small things. What other questions does this bring up in your detoured walk with God? What question keeps coming back? What question or unexplained event is standing between you and God?

THE SIZE OF LOSS

4. Was there a time you felt a profound sense of loss over something relatively small?

5. Looking back, how did God become part of the smallness of your life?

6. How would your faith be stronger if you knew God knows and cares about every loss, regardless of the size? How would that look in your life?

GO DEEPER

Read Matthew 11:28.

DAY 13

What Lasts Forever

Just as surely as we are finite, we are also infinite. We will live forever somewhere. So that "use by" date stamped on our foreheads is a form of God's mercy. And a call to invest in eternity by buying into Him and others.

1. What is the most challenging takeaway from "What Lasts Forever"?

2. How does "What Lasts Forever" help you answer the life question, Is this life all there is?

NAVIGATING YOUR OWN DIVINE DETOUR

3. "What Lasts Forever" explored the Question of Worry as it relates to the finitude of physical life. What other questions does this bring up in your detoured walk with God? What question keeps coming back? What question or unexplained event is standing between you and God?

WHAT LASTS FOREVER

4. Was there a time you felt pulled into believing this world will go on forever?

5. Looking back, how did God help you realize that you don't want this world to last indefinitely?

6. How would your faith be stronger if you knew God intended for only our love for Him and for others to last? How would that look in your life?

GO DEEPER

Read Matthew 6:20, 22:37-40.

DAY 14

Surviving a Collapse

When it feels like all is gone, you can only fall so far. Jesus never promised it won't be painful, but He did promise a threshould in the Father's arms.

1. What is the most challenging takeaway from "Surviving a Collapse"?

2. How does "Surviving a Collapse" help you answer the life question, Is God always good?

3. "Surviving a Collapse" explored the Question of Doubt as it relates to protection when life falls apart. What other questions does this bring up in your detoured walk with God? What question keeps coming back? What question or unexplained event is standing between you and God?

SURVIVING A COLLAPSE

4. Was there a time you felt the rug pulled out from under you?

5. Looking back, how did God provide a threshold for you?

6. How would your faith be stronger if you knew God only allows you to fall so far? How would that look in your life?

GO DEEPER

Read Matthew 7:24, Ezra 6:3.

DAY 15

A Prodigal's Parent

True to the Bible's overarching theme of exile and homecoming, the prodigal parable is the saga of the entire human race. But perhaps most importantly, it is the story of God's long-suffering, His patient plan to bring us all home.

1. What is the most challenging takeaway from "A Prodigal's Parent"?

2. How does "A Prodigal's Parent" help you answer the life question, Is God always good?

NAVIGATING YOUR OWN DIVINE DETOUR

3. "A Prodigal's Parent" explored the Question of Doubt as it relates to our wandering from God. What other questions does this bring up in your detoured walk with God? What question keeps coming back? What question or unexplained event is standing between you and God?

4. Was there a time you felt a long way off from God?

5. Looking back, how did God demonstrate His patience and long-suffering?

6. How would your faith be stronger if you knew God continually scans the horizon, waiting for us to come home? How would that look in your life?

GO DEEPER

Read Luke 15:20, 24.

DAY 16

What Love Looks Like

H*esed* is a never-going-to-leave-you kind of love. Like God showed from Eden to Calvary. Like my parents did for over six decades, even when I didn't always see it.

1. What is the most challenging takeaway from "What Love Looks Like"?

2. How does "What Love Looks Like" help you answer the life question, Is God always good?

NAVIGATING YOUR OWN DIVINE DETOUR

3. "What Love Looks Like" explored the Question of Doubt as it relates to God's loyal love. What other questions does this bring up in your detoured walk with God? What question keeps coming back? What question or unexplained event is standing between you and God?

4. Was there a time you felt unloved by God?

5. Looking back, how did God show His commitment through continual, everyday blessings?

6. How would your faith be stronger if you knew God works through the promise-keeping loyalty of others? How would that look in your life?

GO DEEPER

Read Exodus 34:6.

DAY 17

Adjusting the Font Size

We all know God seems not to intervene at times of our greatest need. Those days when we can only perceive our circumstance through helplessness, we are perhaps experiencing our situation in its truest form. Seeing this world through the refraction of our human tears allows for the rainbows to take shape in our own lives. And those rainbows are promises.

1. What is the most challenging takeaway from "Adjusting the Font Size"?

2. How does "Adjusting the Font Size" help you answer the life question, Is God always good?

NAVIGATING YOUR OWN DIVINE DETOUR

3. "Adjusting the Font Size" explored the Question of Doubt as it relates to not seeing God's hand move. What other questions does this bring up in your detoured walk with God? What question keeps coming back? What question or unexplained event is standing between you and God?

ADJUSTING THE FONT SIZE

4. Was there a time you felt unable to see God working in the details of your life?

5. Looking back, how did God work small things toward a bigger, better end?

6. How would your faith be stronger if you knew God never allows our circumstances to destroy us? How would that look in your life?

GO DEEPER

Read Genesis 9:11.

DAY 18

Mundane Matters

The God of the miraculous is the God of the ordinary. And perhaps He is most present in the everyday moments of our lives. His humble, common beginning positioned Him to infiltrate and redeem every insignificant moment.

1. What is the most challenging takeaway from "Mundane Matters"?

2. How does "Mundane Matters" help you answer the life question, Is God always good?

3. "Mundane Matters" explored the Question of Doubt as it relates to His everyday care. What other questions does this bring up in your detoured walk with God? What question keeps coming back? What question or unexplained event is standing between you and God?

4. Was there a time you felt God was absent from the mundane parts of your life?

5. Looking back, how did God consistently and faithfully work in your everyday scenes?

6. How would your faith be stronger if you knew God is most present in the mundane moments of our lives? How would that look in your life?

GO DEEPER

Read Exodus 16:4–5.

DAY 19

Mosquitoes, Martians, and a Trustworthy God

Although God is always good and trustworthy, He never said our lives would be. In fact, He said just the opposite. But this trustworthy God never gave up on rescuing us from an untrustworthy world.

1. What is the most challenging takeaway from "Mosquitoes, Martians, and a Trustworthy God"?

2. How does "Mosquitoes, Martians, and a Trustworthy God" help you answer the life question, Is God always good?

NAVIGATING YOUR OWN DIVINE DETOUR

3. "Mosquitoes, Martians, and a Trustworthy God" explored the Question of Doubt as it relates to trusting God in an untrustworthy world. What other questions does this bring up in your detoured walk with God? What question keeps coming back? What question or unexplained event is standing between you and God?

4. Was there a time you felt misled by God about receiving His blessings in life?

5. Looking back, how did God provide grace and peace in a bad situation?

6. How would your faith be stronger if you knew God warned us life would be difficult, but He would redeem it? How would that look in your life?

GO DEEPER

Read Ecclesiastes 4:1, Romans 8:28.

DAY 20

Both Sides of Water

Water's two sides are the full picture of God's plan to bring us close to Him. He knew we'd have to feel the rising water to need a rescue. He knew grace would mean nothing if we aren't saved from anything. He knew we'd have to experience hopelessness to appreciate holiness.

1. What is the most challenging takeaway from "Both Sides of Water"?

2. How does "Both Sides of Water" help you answer the life question, Is God always good?

NAVIGATING YOUR OWN DIVINE DETOUR

3. "Both Sides of Water" explored the Question of Doubt as it relates to being saved from the floods of life. What other questions does this bring up in your detoured walk with God? What question keeps coming back? What question or unexplained event is standing between you and God?

4. Was there a time you felt swept away by swift and powerful circumstances?

5. Looking back, how did God bring dependence on Him from that experience?

6. How would your faith be stronger if you knew God uses setbacks to firm up salvation? How would that look in your life?

GO DEEPER

Read Psalm 69:1, Isaiah 12:3.

DAY 21

A Lapse of Faith

Lapses can cause our faith to be suspended in time. And yet in that space, God actually buttresses our belief into something stronger than it would have been otherwise, able to face whatever the next may be.

1. What is the most challenging takeaway from "A Lapse of Faith"?

2. How does "A Lapse of Faith" help you answer the life question, Is God always good?

NAVIGATING YOUR OWN DIVINE DETOUR

3. "A Lapse of Faith" explored the Question of Doubt as it relates to periods of uncertainty in faith. What other questions does this bring up in your detoured walk with God? What question keeps coming back? What question or unexplained event is standing between you and God?

A LAPSE OF FAITH

4. Was there a time you felt an expansive divide between you and God?

5. Looking back, how did God send an answer to bridge your faith lapse?

6. How would your faith be stronger if you knew God understands lapses in belief? How would that look in your life?

GO DEEPER

Read Matthew 11:3.

DAY 22

Recency Syndrome

Sometimes in a faithful life, circumstances get worse, not better. Faith in God's future grace for us, in His long-term plan, is what sustains us in those desperate moments. The challenge is to remember the entire story, not just the part we're living. Maybe it takes all the chapters, not just the most recent ones, for the story to make sense.

1. What is the most challenging takeaway from "Recency Syndrome"?

2. How does "Recency Syndrome" help you answer the life question, Is God always good?

NAVIGATING YOUR OWN DIVINE DETOUR

3. "Recency Syndrome" explored the Question of Doubt as it relates to a recent unresolved crisis. What other questions does this bring up in your detoured walk with God? What question keeps coming back? What question or unexplained event is standing between you and God?

RECENCY SYNDROME

4. Was there a time you felt like judging God's character by how recently He'd answered a prayer in your favor?

5. Looking back, how did God take that experience from crisis to crown?

6. How would your faith be stronger if you knew God is the God of the long-term? How would that look in your life?

GO DEEPER

Read Genesis 50:20.

DAY 23

Locust Years

Our God is unbound by time. He can completely redeem both our past and our future. God works everything together to restore what sin and a broken world have cost us.

1. What is the most challenging takeaway from "Locust Years"?

2. How does "Locust Years" help you answer the life question, Is God always good?

NAVIGATING YOUR OWN DIVINE DETOUR

3. "Locust Years" explored the Question of Doubt as it relates to past regret and future uncertainty. What other questions does this bring up in your detoured walk with God? What question keeps coming back? What question or unexplained event is standing between you and God?

LOCUST YEARS

4. Was there a time you felt marred by your past or robbed of a future?

5. Looking back, how did God restore those years?

6. How would your faith be stronger if you knew God promised to redeem both the past and the future? How would that look in your life?

GO DEEPER

Read Joel 2:25.

DAY 24

Languishing & Loaned Words

The way out of the stranglehold of languishing is with something called flourishing. Flourishing only happens with a renewed focus, concentrating on something outside ourselves.

1. What is the most challenging takeaway from "Languishing & Loaned Words"?

2. How does "Languishing & Loaned Words" help you answer the life question, Is God always good?

3. "Languishing & Loaned Words" explored the Question of Doubt as it relates to being emotionally and spiritually stuck. What other questions does this bring up in your detoured walk with God? What question keeps coming back? What question or unexplained event is standing between you and God?

4. Was there a time you felt trapped somewhere in a tight place or in an uncomfortable circumstance?

5. Looking back, how did God remind you of what you knew to be true about Him?

6. How would your faith be stronger if you knew God's heart is constant? How would that look in your life?

GO DEEPER

Read Psalm 52:8–9.

DAY 25

In the Shadow of a Stump

Scripture never promises we won't experience the worst the world has to offer. But it does promise that when we do, we won't be overtaken and we won't be alone. Sometimes the shadowy darkness is more about being taken care of in the middle of the unanticipated.

1. What is the most challenging takeaway from "In the Shadow of a Stump?"

2. How does "In the Shadow of a Stump" help you answer the life question, Is God always good?

NAVIGATING YOUR OWN DIVINE DETOUR

3. "In the Shadow of a Stump" explored the Question of Doubt as it relates to our identity. What other questions does this bring up in your detoured walk with God? What question keeps coming back? What question or unexplained event is standing between you and God?

4. Was there a time you felt like you were living in the shadow of something negative?

5. Looking back, how did God provide shelter in that dark place?

6. How would your faith be stronger if you knew God sometimes uses shadows for protection? How would that look in your life?

GO DEEPER

Read Psalm 36:7.

DAY 26

Finding Answers in Unanswered Prayers

When our own prayers feel unanswered, it might be that God wants something different for us. And when He does, it's always something better. For our good and for His glory. We are wrapped together in that dual eternal purpose.

1. What is the most challenging takeaway from "Finding Answers in Unanswered Prayers"?

2. How does "Finding Answers in Unanswered Prayers" help you answer the life question, Is God always good?

NAVIGATING YOUR OWN DIVINE DETOUR

3. "Finding Answers in Unanswered Prayers" explored the Question of Doubt as it relates to prayers that seem unanswered. What other questions does this bring up in your detoured walk with God? What question keeps coming back? What question or unexplained event is standing between you and God?

FINDING ANSWERS IN UNANSWERED PRAYERS

4. Was there a time you felt ignored or dismissed by God?

5. Looking back, how did God answer your prayer in a way you didn't expect?

6. How would your faith be stronger if you knew God often protects us and ultimately glorifies Himself through unanswered prayers? How would that look in your life?

GO DEEPER

Read John 11:1–6, 14–15, 41–44.

DAY 27

A Better Memory

Some of what we should remember is good: family celebrations, God's provision, healings, peace. But some of what we need to recall is painful: death, periods of need, illness, strife. It all shapes us and draws us into a deeper understanding of God's world and our place in it.

1. What is the most challenging takeaway from "A Better Memory"?

2. How does "A Better Memory" help you answer the life question, Is God's plan enough?

3. "A Better Memory" explored the Question of Control as it relates to past hardships and future challenges. What other questions does this bring up in your detoured walk with God? What question keeps coming back? What question or unexplained event is standing between you and God?

4. Was there a time you felt a desire to erase your hard memories?

5. Looking back, how did God tap into those memories to build trust in Him?

6. How would your faith be stronger if you knew God uses both good and bad moments to deepen your understanding of His care? How would that look in your life?

GO DEEPER

Read Psalm 143:5, Romans 15:15.

DAY 28

Getting Okay with Giving Up

Relinquishment is not an everyday prayer. It is not the first prayer we pray, but it might be the last. It comes only after we've petitioned tirelessly. We have to get to the point past desperation. We have to be prepared to give up the very thing we value most for God's greater planned good.

1. What is the most challenging takeaway from "Getting Okay with Giving Up"?

2. How does "Getting Okay with Giving Up" help you answer the life question, Is God's plan enough?

NAVIGATING YOUR OWN DIVINE DETOUR

3. "Getting Okay with Giving Up" explored the Question of Control as it relates to trust in God's better plan. What other questions does this bring up in your detoured walk with God? What question keeps coming back? What question or unexplained event is standing between you and God?

GETTING OKAY WITH GIVING UP

4. Was there a time you felt bent in two over an ongoing prayerful request?

5. Looking back, how did God urge you toward relinquishing it?

6. How would your faith be stronger if you knew God might wait for our relinquishment to open up another part of His plan for us? How would that look in your life?

GO DEEPER

Read Ecclesiastes 3:6, Luke 22:42.

DAY 29

When God Disappoints

We can't expect what God never promised, but we can always expect what He did. He doesn't promise to save us from life's suffering, but He does promise to use our suffering to eventually produce hope.

1. What is the most challenging takeaway from "When God Disappoints"?

2. How does "When God Disappoints" help you answer the life question, Is God's plan enough?

3. "When God Disappoints" explored the Question of Control as it relates to disappoinment in life. What other questions does this bring up in your detoured walk with God? What question keeps coming back? What question or unexplained event is standing between you and God?

4. Was there a time you felt a need to reshape God's promises into your own expectations?

5. Looking back, how did God keep His promise, despite your unmet expectation?

6. How would your faith be stronger if you knew God doesn't promise protection from suffering but rather a newfound hope? How would that look in your life?

GO DEEPER

Read Romans 5:3–4.

DAY 30

Trust Enough to Surrender

We first have to lay down what's in our hand—we have to surrender our own strength to gain His. We must do what we can but leave the final result in God's hands. In doing this, we begin to realize what God wanted us to know all along: The outcome doesn't depend on our power or ability but His.

1. What is the most challenging takeaway from "Trust Enough to Surrender"?

2. How does "Trust Enough to Surrender" help you answer the life question, Is God's plan enough?

NAVIGATING YOUR OWN DIVINE DETOUR

3. "Trust Enough to Surrender" explored the Question of Control as it relates to letting go of a struggle. What other questions does this bring up in your detoured walk with God? What question keeps coming back? What question or unexplained event is standing between you and God?

4. Was there a time you felt compelled to continue a battle you couldn't win?

5. Looking back, how did God demonstrate His power through your lack of power?

6. How would your faith be stronger if you knew God intends for the battle to be His, not ours? How would that look in your life?

GO DEEPER

Read Exodus 14:14.

DAY 31

Sitting on the Bus

Waiting builds dependency on God. When God says wait, He is saying, cling to Me. Rather than on an outcome or a result. He puts Himself above the request, which helps us see that He is our only lasting hope.

1. What is the most challenging takeaway from "Sitting on the Bus"?

2. How does "Sitting on the Bus" help you answer the life question, Is God's plan enough?

3. "Sitting on the Bus" explored the Question of Control as it relates to waiting. What other questions does this bring up in your detoured walk with God? What question keeps coming back? What question or unexplained event is standing between you and God?

4. Was there a time you felt God would never show up in your life?

5. Looking back, how did God build dependency on Him through that drawn-out trial?

6. How would your faith be stronger if you knew God uses waiting time to refocus our desire away from the result and toward Him? How would that look in your life?

GO DEEPER

Read Matthew 28:20.

DAY 32

Not What We Expected

From the desert manna to Sarah's child to a donkey-riding King, *not what we expected* is how our God works. And it's how He loves. Despite our limited understanding, whether we know it or not, we live every day bound tight in this unpredictable love.

1. What is the most challenging takeaway from "Not What We Expected"?

2. How does "Not What We Expected" help you answer the life question, Is God's plan enough?

NAVIGATING YOUR OWN DIVINE DETOUR

3. "Not What We Expected" explored the Question of Control as it relates to unmet expectations. What other questions does this bring up in your detoured walk with God? What question keeps coming back? What question or unexplained event is standing between you and God?

4. Was there a time you felt a deep need being unmet by God?

5. Looking back, how did God work in that situation despite your lack of understanding?

6. How would your faith be stronger if you knew God often challenges our expectations to reveal His better plan? How would that look in your life?

GO DEEPER

Read Exodus 33:14, Luke 19:29–38.

DAY 33

In Between

As God-followers, we are charged to live the story, trusting Him to finish it. And sometimes that means hanging out for a while in between, in liminal space. Liminal space is a place of not knowing. It is where faith lives.

1. What is the most challenging takeaway from "In Between"?

2. How does "In Between" help you answer the life question, Is God's plan enough?

3. "In Between" explored the Question of Control as it relates to living in liminal space. What other questions does this bring up in your detoured walk with God? What question keeps coming back? What question or unexplained event is standing between you and God?

4. Was there a time you felt stuck between two points of existence?

5. Looking back, how did God finish the story you were living?

6. How would your faith be stronger if you knew God uses liminal space as a point of entry to something new? How would that look in your life?

GO DEEPER

Read Ruth 2:23.

DAY 34

Midrace Joy

Midrace joy is an act of celebrating the life we have and accepting whatever is ahead that we cannot see. The dark middle days are where we trust He's not just a Healer, He's a Resurrector.

1. What is the most challenging takeaway from "Midrace Joy"?

2. How does "Midrace Joy" help you answer the life question, Is God's plan enough?

NAVIGATING YOUR OWN DIVINE DETOUR

3. "Midrace Joy" explored the Question of Control as it relates to ongoing issues in life. What other questions does this bring up in your detoured walk with God? What question keeps coming back? What question or unexplained event is standing between you and God?

4. Was there a time you felt like you were running an endurance race in life?

5. Looking back, how did God come alongside you and offer bits of joy?

6. How would your faith be stronger if you knew God never leaves us to run the long course alone? How would that look in your life?

GO DEEPER

Read 2 Corinthians 1:9, Philippians 3:8.

DAY 35

Making Mistakes

We mistake-averse believers must know that the only way we can stop the mistakes is to stop living. But we also know a God with a pretty impressive résumé of turning broken into beautiful—doubt to truth, darkness to light, death to life. His touch can create the opposite of what should be.

1. What is the most challenging takeaway from "Making Mistakes"?

2. How does "Making Mistakes" help you answer the life question, Is God's plan enough?

NAVIGATING YOUR OWN DIVINE DETOUR

3. "Making Mistakes" explored the Question of Control as it relates to failure. What other questions does this bring up in your detoured walk with God? What question keeps coming back? What question or unexplained event is standing between you and God?

MAKING MISTAKES

4. Was there a time you felt you had made a mistake that couldn't be corrrected?

5. Looking back, how did God turn it into the opposite of what it should be?

6. How would your faith be stronger if you knew God sees us as more beautiful and useful in His Kingdom with our imperfections and breaking points defined? How would that look in your life?

GO DEEPER

Read Jonah 2.

DAY 36

Parented by Porchlight

We all need Someone who, from a foggy distance, we can still see. But darkness has to roll in or we never know the importance of the light source. Rather than saving us from the storms, God prepares us to handle them.

1. What is the most challenging takeaway from "Parented by Porch Light"?

2. How does "Parented by Porch Light" help you answer the life question, Is God's plan enough?

NAVIGATING YOUR OWN DIVINE DETOUR

3. "Parented by Porch Light" explored the Question of Control as it relates to grace and rescue. What other questions does this bring up in your detoured walk with God? What question keeps coming back? What question or unexplained event is standing between you and God?

4. Was there a time you felt God could have intervened and didn't?

5. Looking back, how did God allow you to see His light more clearly in the dark?

6. How would your faith be stronger if you knew God doesn't always rescue us from life's storms, but always prepares us to handle them? How would that look in your life?

GO DEEPER

Read Exodus 13:21–22, Matthew 2:9.

DAY 37

Conquering the Stairs

Whatever we are facing, we can confidently give the frightening elevations to our all-knowing God. We will never find ourselves in a place He hasn't been. In a situation He doesn't know. In a circumstance He doesn't control.

1. What is the most challenging takeaway from "Conquering the Stairs"?

2. How does "Conquering the Stairs" help you answer the life question, Is God's plan enough?

NAVIGATING YOUR OWN DIVINE DETOUR

3. "Conquering the Stairs" explored the Question of Control as it relates to tackling the unknown. What other questions does this bring up in your detoured walk with God? What question keeps coming back? What question or unexplained event is standing between you and God?

CONQUERING THE STAIRS

4. Was there a time you felt paralyzed by fear of the unknown?

5. Looking back, how did God get you through that frightening time?

6. How would your faith be stronger if you knew God always sits at the top of the stairs He asks us to climb? How would that look in your life?

GO DEEPER

Read Job 3:25, 1 John 4:18.

DAY 38

When Doors Close

A closed door may clear the way for something more important for us to do or for a greater plan to begin unfolding. Without God's full explanation, we have to keep going to get to the perfect door. And bypass all the less-than-perfect closed ones. Closed doors can actually be more gracious than open ones.

1. What is the most challenging takeaway from "When Doors Close"?

2. How does "When Doors Close" help you answer the life question, Is God's plan enough?

NAVIGATING YOUR OWN DIVINE DETOUR

3. "When Doors Close" explored the Question of Control as it relates to lost opportunities. What other questions does this bring up in your detoured walk with God? What question keeps coming back? What question or unexplained event is standing between you and God?

4. Was there a time you felt on the locked-out side of a door you wish would open?

5. Looking back, how did God provide a better door?

6. How would your faith be stronger if you knew God uses closed doors as a way of protection? How would that look in your life?

GO DEEPER

Read Revelation 3:8, Matthew 25:21.

DAY 39

A Desperate Reach

Reaching says we can't do this on our own. Reaching is the very act of believing.

1. What is the most challenging takeaway from "A Desperate Reach"?

2. How does "A Desperate Reach" help you answer the life question, Is God's plan enough?

NAVIGATING YOUR OWN DIVINE DETOUR

3. "A Desperate Reach" explored the Question of Control as it relates to vulnerability in despair. What other questions does this bring up in your detoured walk with God? What question keeps coming back? What question or unexplained event is standing between you and God?

A DESPERATE REACH

4. Was there a time you felt desperate in a situation and reached out to God?

5. Looking back, how did God provide a clearer view of Himself?

6. How would your faith be stronger if you knew God uses a reach to turn our hearts to Him? How would that look in your life?

GO DEEPER

Read Matthew 9:20–22.

DAY 40

A Charge to Keep Questioning

While Satan wants to use questions to separate us from God, the Spirit intends to use them to bring us closer to Him. Just as Jesus's painful time in the desert launched his history-defining ministry, the days in the desert can refresh your faith and revamp your story.

1. Summarize your unanswered questions below, and add to this list as they come up:

NAVIGATING YOUR OWN DIVINE DETOUR

2. What steps can you take to embrace these questions? Who/what else would this involve? How would this look in your life?

A CHARGE TO KEEP QUESTIONING

A PLEDGE TO CONTINUE THE JOURNEY

My job is to never stop asking the hard questions, to engage in the faith struggles, and to trust the detours to the God who can handle it all.

The God who gives me an eternal perspective to overcome my worries.

The God who has already proven He is the God of boundless love and trustworthiness.

The God whose long-term perspective and plan far overshadow my own.

I will expect the detours. And most importantly, I will keep asking the questions. They will keep my faith alive.

Signed: _____

Date: _____

About the Author

Lori Ann Wood lives in the shadow of the Ozark Mountains in beautiful Bentonville, Arkansas, with her husband, the unsuspecting guy she chased all the way from ninth grade to grad school. She is mom to three world-changing young adults, one impressive son-in-law (who all live too far away) and a miniature dachshund named Pearl (who threatens to never leave). Her newest obsession is her granddaughter Hazel.

Lori Ann is a WomenHeart Champion Community Educator and an American Heart Association Ambassador. She also serves on the Blog Contributor Team for *The Joyful Life Magazine*. In addition to receiving the Frederick Buechner Narrative Essay Award and awards from the Colorado Christian Writers and the Evangelical Press Association, her work has been published in numerous print journals including *The Christian Century Magazine, Just Between Us Magazine, The Joyful Life Magazine, Bella Grace Magazine, Heart Insight Magazine, Sweet to the Soul FAITH Magazine,* and *Truly Magazine*. Her articles have also appeared on websites such as *The New York Times, Pepperdine University Press, Yahoo Lifestyle, MSN,* and *NewsFlash,* and on blogs including *Women | Faith & Story, Kindred Mom, WomenHeart,* and *The Mighty.*

But Lori Ann has not always been a writer.

A life detour reordered her priorities and rattled her faith.

In 2015, despite otherwise pristine health, Lori Ann almost died from heart failure from an unknown cause.

Having discovered this chronic, progressive condition almost too late, Lori Ann now writes to encourage difficult faith questions along the detours of life. Her passion is to connect with readers and help them hold onto their faith when they find themselves on a path they didn't choose.

Get her free guide for staying close to God in hard times at https://loriannwood.com/hope.

Answers, gifts... love and promises...

Abba's Devotion series

Available in bookstores and online retailers.

www.crossrivermedia.com

If you enjoyed this book, will you consider sharing it with others?

- Please mention the book on Facebook, Instagram, Pinterest, or another social media site.

- Recommend this book to your small group, book club, and workplace.

- Head over to Facebook.com/CrossRiverMedia, 'Like' the page and post a comment as to what you enjoyed the most.

- Pick up a copy for someone you know who would be challenged or encouraged by this message.

- Write a review on your favorite ebook platform.

- To learn about our latest releases subscribe to our newsletter at CrossRiverMedia.com.

www.ingramcontent.com/pod-product-compliance
Lightning Source LLC
Chambersburg PA
CBHW070850050426
42453CB00012B/2128